Set within a splintered hyperreality, F
prosaic poems dealing with the 'ghost
with the world we have created for o
trauma of human detachment, and fo
culture, the author pins open our eyes
falsified, disconnected and disposed
a distinct angularity, this series of
with the unreal, and the material nature of existence. Upon absorption,
readers become transparent, translucent; ghosts not only of ourselves, but of
the twisted humanity we find ourselves sleepwalking into.

— Stuart McPherson, *Obligate Carnivore*

Ghost Clinic began, and is perhaps destined to remain, an inscrutable factory.
A place to launder the dead.' Like a hypnotist's command, the opening lines
of Nathaniel King's searing debut of lyrical essays plunges us into a surreal
twilight world; one uncannily reminiscent of our own. *Ghost Clinic* dares us to
consider the absurd rituals and obsessions that haunt contemporary existence.
Following an unlikely yet carefully curated cast: a celebrity avatar visited by the
apparition of his former agent, a rotten apple delivering a prophecy, Claude
Monet's late wife, King skilfully disseminates meaning. His protagonists
stumble half-awake through a dying epoch, plagued by the symptoms of
their psychic ills, yet unable to fully grasp what is happening to them. While
often absurd in the forms they take, their crises of meaning and alienation
feels uncomfortably close to home. Weaponizing wry humour, King delivers
his weightiest provocations as punchlines. It's through this sleight of hand
that his inquiries materialise like poltergeists: is language a tool to create or
obfuscate reality? Just how far have we strayed from paradise? Both a haunting
meditation on our cultural moment, and a luminous chronicle of the ghosts
that stalk the waking world, *Ghost Clinic* marks the entrance of a significant
new talent.

— Steve Mallon, *Iced Lemon Water*

There's lots I could say about this beautiful book: King's writing bears an almost
Augustan affinity with exacting allusivity, pronunciamento and a wit that hits
like exercise at great altitudes: swabbing the saliva of mystification from your
brow before inspecting all manner of post-nostalgic detritus — what (un)
life are we on, now? Deftly dispersing rather than denying docu-narrative
elements, *Ghost Clinic* also accommodates Objectivist precision, epigrammatic
bite, meta-fictional incursions and a self-teasing resistance to falling back hard
on the ego-expressivist base of poetic orthodoxy — even when wrestling with
ambiguous loss. A chink of ice against received lyric feeling awakens another
witness to the revenants demanding a reckoning for a message missed amid
the systemic polis-rot. Look beyond the cloud of second-hand ice cream vape,
tender skeptic; though there's never a guarantee you'll feel the 'sweet switch
of the body' like Berryman's Henry, you'll be sharing in something 'dripping
with devotion'.

— I. S. Rowley, *The Undeliverable*

GHOST CLINIC

Nathaniel King is a poet from Cornwall, UK. He holds an MSc in Creative Writing from The University of Edinburgh and currently lives and teaches in London.

ISBN: 978-1-915079-61-9

Cover designed by Aaron Kent

Edited and typeset by Aaron Kent

Broken Sleep Books Ltd
Rhydwen,
Talgarreg,
SA44 4HB
Wales

Contents

Ghost Clinic

Nathaniel King

This horror will grow mild, this darkness light.
— John Milton, *Paradise Lost*

I

1. Ghost Clinic began, and is perhaps destined to remain, an inscrutable factory. A place to launder the dead. A rumour of emancipation. *Ghost Clinic* is an overexposed photograph of a vanishing empire. Its inhabitants range from the lawless to the phosphorescent, the terminally ill to those remembered as tantalising provocations. One might step over the threshold and be welcomed as an estranged friend, or else, like a cool hand drifting over a cylindrical bottle of warm white bees, lose themself to its shadowy machinations. *Ghost Clinic* has been missing, privatised, sold off in discrete fragments to the highest bidder. Like a doppelganger engaged in chess, it remains only to be played in the right combination.

2. In 2019, the NHS registered 3.6 million more patients in their systems than there were people in England. This discrepancy prompted an independent review and investigation into what were deemed 'ghost clinics', by an outside organisation tasked with uncovering the truth behind the identities of these so-called ghost patients. A spokesperson for the British Medical Association claimed this anomaly could be accounted for by patients who had recently died, those who had emigrated or left the country, and many who were homeless or simply unaccounted for in government statistics. What was unconditionally ruled out however was wilful deception by hard-working GPs. Doctors, on average, received £150 per patient in 2019. The team have since estimated that up to £88m may be being incorrectly claimed for - around 1% of the GP budget. Like a mechanical goldfinch in a dead man's palm, how can we reclaim this divinity?

3. Like birds, we create sublimity from the raw materials of our neighbourhood. Claude Monet, recalling his wife on her deathbed, found himself "staring at her tragic countenance, automatically trying to identify the sequence, the proportion of light and shade in the colours that death had imposed on the immobile face." His life partner, in her final moments, reduced irrevocably to aesthetic potential. We cannot choose how we remember. "In spite of myself, my reflexes drew me into the unconscious operation that is but the daily order of my life." Camille, devoted wife of nine years, trapped eternally in a daguerreotype of ice, of her husband's making. An image fed back to us through layers of distortion. Her expression is serene, resigned, cocooned in huge webs of atrophied snow. Often deemed 'the muse who escaped oblivion'. Like Monet, I too am trying to seduce your absence down from orbit, into something I can wield: a light bone of language, a painting knife for carving out space between ghosts and goldfinches.

4. In ancient Japanese culture, ghosts, known as 'Yūre', have no feet. If you pick up a comb, you will pick up suffering. Saliva in the brow will stop the fox bewitching you. Many superstitions persist. Their presence can be intimated by lighting two candles near a jasmine lily and closing your eyes. I spend the night like this, engrossed in mesmerising falsehoods.

5. We are each gifted with an incurable obsession. Some sudden exit by the wrong door. You can rub a whale's heart across a windowpane to reveal its ambergris. You can dedicate yourself to an occupation so completely empty as to experience weightlessness. It's only a metaphysical wound, a trick of the light.

6. At the height of nationwide lockdown, sheetless ghosts appeared in the *Wendy's* parking lot, demanding, without irony, ultimate absolution—their sins designed by algorithms and sporting modern, androgynous haircuts. The spectacle of their limitless pain was salubrious, life-giving. *Wendy's* began to mimic the reign of an ancient monarch, baptising their vast network of congregants in holy water, extracted from a mountain-spring where fallen cheerleaders had recently bathed. Across a crowded interface of grief, an island of intermittent connection emerged. Strangers swam through layers of polluted o-zone to touch one another's faces. Football players traded two bars of service for forgiveness. The sanctity of the drive-thru was total: a confession booth bedecked in bullet-proof glass. As their grip on suburbia tightened, ghosts from nearby towns began to orbit the restaurant, in star-spangled convertibles curtained by twilight. Soon there were too many to rescue. The more desperate ghosts made offerings: a care package of tender nudes, a wooden stake doused in Salem fog, a family photo album with the faces carefully etched out. Was it antipathy? A sophisticated trend? As the leaves began to turn, local law enforcement became involved. Decrying jingoism, they closed all of *Wendy's'* operations in the area, forcing the ghosts to disperse like dusky sunlight released from a shrouded attic. You can still spot them on crisp October evenings, drifting aimlessly in a vast requiem of nostalgia.

7. I like to imagine a version of the show, *Scrubs,* where Zach Braff has been replaced by a roiling, effervescent vapour. Everybody else is exactly the same. In the first episode, Braff rolls along the corridors of Sacred Heart Hospital, absorbing everything in his path: staff, patients, vending machines. When supporting cast members recite their lines to Braff, he emanates a kind of dark, alien incantation which causes them to dissolve. Their spirits are then exhumed by the cloud, strengthening Braff's hold on Sacred Heart. The nameless janitor, in a moment of mutiny, assembles an elite team of field personnel, known as 'scrubs', who spend the remainder of the series attempting to rid the hospital of this malign plague. Every episode is set to the opening salvo of 'How to Save a Life' by popular noughties sock-rock band, *The Fray.* A mid-season cliff-hanger features Eliot declaring her love to the vapour. As he begins to chant menacingly, the screen fades to black.

8. Sylvia is perched on the diving board. Alice checks her phone into purgatory. Stephanie removes her air pods while walking through the library quad. Annette has this one thought carved into a block yet in a sentence there is nowhere for it to hide. Sarah impressed upon us the need for truth in art, or, failing that, absolute deception. In everything they did, they erred towards caution, towards formal elegance. The reporter chinks ice against the receiver and hangs up.

9. In fruit-tree shade by the church gate, mourners gather to exchange fleshless, ephemeral data. The December air crackles with frost. A rotten apple is presented from inside a heavy garment, an augur of mischief. From its lips, a strange melody floats upward like burned incense. *The entire imaginative life of individuals stubbornly persists to live by the old magical notions.* What did it just say? *You have succumbed to an ontological obsession with psychic realms, and exist in a liminal state between waking life and death.* Seriously, who's doing that? The mourners, expecting a miracle which had been stubbornly denied, became increasingly unnerved by the apple's testament. *Your world is one of stubborn recurrence, of sacred images and sacrifice, a numinous landscape inhabited by demons and strange beasts.* Dreading further exposure, they quickly scattered across the moors, disturbed by their encounter with this reanimated sear. *There is, however, a vast difference between these psychic worlds and the worlds of antiquity. A constellation of quasi-religious fervour emerges...* The apple continued its luminous prophecy long into the dawn.

10. We expected dawn to flush, scatter on high-rises, pinkening safehouses and public libraries. We expected to meditate on the 'facts' alone: evoking the law wherever possible. We gave up our neighbours. We guessed their star signs, conspiring proudly against the zodiac. Night was a passing conflict in which biography was raised to the status of myth. Whenever a marble was conspicuously dropped, we passed through cemeteries of culpability. We were waiting for one raw encounter. One moment where our purpose was made manifest. We gave up our spouses, finding it preferable to record flocks of geese in a dark mirror. The anatomy of a cloud was studied by candlelight. Two sets of twins, separated by a fascination with herd immunity, had reconciled upon sharing a pink premonition, a gradual softening of dawn. Coming from a long line of tailors, we failed to distinguish between our own buttons and those of our ancestors. An investigation was commenced to determine the exact shade of our souls, while all pursuits deemed enfeebling (reading, writing, drawing) were outlawed. By the time we considered giving ourselves up, our apartments had been ransacked of colour. The ice-cold milk jug, bereft of memories, shed a single tear. We savoured the sweetness of a ritual since then unknown to us, like prisoners with a delicious secret, and retreated once more into shadow—a place without the possibility of pink.

interludes

Synthia calls home
from the edge of the infinity pool
chinking ice against the receiver
takes a small knife
to the soft rind of a citrus plant
surrounded by references
that can't touch her

today she felt
raw & unloved
like a cursed e-mail chain
still dreaming about
black & white furbies
soft as couture

drinking arctic water
on a california balcony
locus of palm trees
& suicidal ideation
blood-red vine tomatoes
waving goodbye from the beds
of distant pick-up trucks

                    nothing is sacred
          except for rare celebrity sightings
                 imagine being the person
                    who develops a photo
                        of keanu reeves
               crying on a rollercoaster

why does the internet always
sound like a funeral
like arthur russell deep cuts
disconsolate anthem
queued on the bluetooth speaker

          synthia applies an exclusive fragrance
             prepared by coco chanel's ghost
                    sage geranium jasmine
                      plus bottled mist
                  from funhouse mirrors

II

11. If you could be anyone living or dead, keep it secret. Sometimes it is too bright to get a haircut so you walk around admiring the clouds & their cumulus trails. You visit *Central Perk*. Across the imported mahogany counter, you hand the waitress blueprints for a spectacular flat-white. Later you pitch her a sitcom called *Ghost Clinic* and present a second blueprint- this time of the director's apartment. Although you donate to the annual benefit, the screenplays don't get any easier. Every single guest star is revealed at once. Various casting directors order them by net-worth. Gunther remains encased in shadow. He is handed a hairless cat. This completes his character arc. Ross becomes lost in the revolving doors. I am drawing nearer to the kind of person who creates elaborate constructions to pave over their personal vacuum. I am feeling about the same as yesterday. I tour the Warner Lot spreading rumours about a *Ghost Clinic* reunion. When I get home, the laughter track sounds slightly more haunted, and nuanced, as if only the sincere fans remain in-studio. This is the one where various disembodied voices are conducting a séance in my apartment.

12. Objectively fantastic conditions for glamping, for networking intimately with lakes and mountains. Sometimes I suspect I'm ghosting you and then discover we're sharing a thermos of scalding hot coffee in the misty, Scottish countryside. Tenderness is an air mattress without the portable pump—it never rises sufficiently for us to reckon with. My only vice is infinite generosity. Give the squirrel some nuts, don't mind if I do. Compliment a babbling brook on its enervating conversation, fuck yeah. Call up *Mountain Rescue* to ask them, and be honest now, do you ever make time to rescue yourselves? It's this travel-sized hairspray that's making me cry. This flushed sunset unfolding delicately beyond the sycamores. While you are low-key storming off, I am trying to gain access to a distant unreachable meadow, to find for you a single pinecone, encrusted with dirt, decay and dripping with devotion.

13. A bundle of corn, wrapped in a studded choke-chain collar, has been deposited through my letterbox. This once belonged to a neighbour's dog, missing since January. He's still out there somewhere. Whoever sent this has the wrong address. Due to the kidnapper's error, a beloved pet, dimly remembered, will be removed from the blue light of a barn. We eat our mistakes, so they say, like ripe cherries staining pristine, white snow. If everyone you ever loved came back at once, could you relinquish your grief? *Fetch*, I say, again and again until various animals begin to materialise on the northern wall of my childhood bedroom. Like if memories are just words we covet, and repeat to ourselves as we brush our teeth, retire to bed, will they soon begin to assume physical form? Outside, as snow keeps falling, dead pets are returning to their adoptive realms. *Fetch*, I say, a single ear of corn in my outstretched hands.

14. The one where Chandler is crying actual tears in the gift wrapped dew. To lighten the mood, he calls his press agent and orders animal balloons to be released into the valley. He tries to locate his car, puffing ice-cream flavoured vape smoke into the atmosphere. Grass hairs stand on end. During a full moon, all that drizzle makes for a great compilation tape. He tries to retrieve his priceless Ray Bans from the soil, where his press agent has buried them before handing in her notice. He looks for an artificial sunrise to drive off into. His press agent appears as an apparition on the hillside, warning Chandler about the price of mercy. It begins to rain crushed Vicodin. No-one told him his life would be this way.

15. In my supernatural research, I came across a review in *Ghost Clinic* which began, with sublime assurance, a comprehensive air of intrigue 'The art of hauntology is amply distinguished from the manufacture of ghosts by the animating presence in the spirit of a fresh idiom; interpreting the stock of available reality by superseding it.' I was never quite the same man after that. I found this critic entirely unknown except in the back issues of a now-defunct quarterly, only available on JSTOR, *The Great Northern Review*. I haunted the message-boards on Reddit, looking for clues, watching reruns of a nineties-sitcom which, for legal reasons, can't be reprinted here. My relationship suffered during this month or so, so did my seminar & lectures, and poems even. To be a Hauntologist, how 'deep' and scientific. I wrote & printed an essay on mid-twentieth century poet, John Berryman, re-deploying all of his key terms and even his sentence structure wherever possible. When the critic answered by Gmail from Stockholm my nervous invitation to come & be honoured at our annual symposium, it must have been ten minutes before I could open my inbox. They arrived in the afternoon, carrying a portmanteau. What struck me most was their complete absence of corporeal form. Upon checking them into the hotel, I returned to my parenthetical translations, and later took a walk in the local botanical gardens, unable to recall their features. On the evening of the critic's reading, I was informed they had checked out of the hotel without leaving a forward address. The details following this are scarce, but for posterity's sake I'll record it here. Apparently, since 2019, this critic had been wilfully deceiving publishers, writing under a variety of false pseudonyms, going so far as to register them at GP clinics to legitimise the existence of their nom-de-plumes. Disturbingly, I continue to be haunted by the memory of their implausibility, their immaculate malpractice.

16. I want to officiate for the songbird in your liver. To offer round-the-clock-surveillance on the soon-to-be. I want to grasp that spirit levitating across the street. Admittedly we had to protect that other small brainless child, life. We stood on the burning deck promising each other everything. We wanted connection at all costs, even if it meant calling up our exes. I'll never leave this place, said the egg yolk to the ovum. Said a crate of miracles falling off the edge of the world. Says me, an out-of-work magician at the harbour. If we ever meet again, let it be as fashionable strangers. A distant hairspray smell recalled in a stranger's apartment. Suitcases pleasurably bumping together in a departures lounge. I want to return here in a hundred years, broken-hearted: an unholy wreck, feeding a note into the vending machine. Please let me hold that beautiful blue ghost, just once.

17. Emergency services have departed this universe. Patient oriented care has been replaced by cubes of synthetic birdsong. When you say take me somewhere sweet, we share a peach in the ICU. The earth is a sublime accommodation, just ask the leaves. We wake up after a ringed night of sensational care, and watch our families hunt for funding in the medicine-green fields. A chiffon pink sunset is burning delicately beyond the sycamores. Before I can speak, you offer me a peach that looks nothing like the memory of peaches. *Take it*, you say, *it's still ripe.*

18. Evening descends upon the clinic. Somebody has sketched a small demon, a Hironimus Bosch in-miniature, in their Sunday newspaper. You wake up uncertain of your surroundings in an easy chair beside the hospital bed. You reach over and adjust the pillow of your companion, who, day by day, steadily slips out of this realm. Snow falls at the glass-blown edge of conscience. Suddenly you recall a luminous canvas in a gallery somewhere years away. As the attendant arrives, you hurriedly sketch a small demon, a Dutch master, with a distinct sense of impending loss.

19. Enclosed is the dawn chorus. Perambulations and exoskeletons. A broadcast from the bottom of a lake. Enclosed is a redacted figure leaving footprints in the snow. A figure 8 turned on its side staring back at you. Hauntology is a portmanteau. A persistence of raw elements from the past. A walk monogrammed with the recurrence of past trauma. It is the sound of a white-hot-forever being erased deliciously, a mechanical goldfinch unfurling in a dead man's palm. Before the telephone rings, the ice melts in the glass. Take it. Listen. Press your palm to the plush-velvet and sense a brief settling of grief. Remember how silent and inviting the refracted light from the *Ghost Clinic* was, how you said it resembled twilight?

20. As the days go by, the great world has grown powerful, and I can no longer drink fragrant shade from the skylight or blissfully step off the balcony. I hold in these hands a gesture of forgetting, like a cantina holds freshwater or a partner holds the door shut to keep out unwanted visitors. Everyone must bear witness or at least witness a witness just once. Take birds for instance, flying low across the frozen lake outside the sanatorium gates. Who asked them to? And the many unlit strangers are competing for your attention today: the plughole drank a spider tomorrow who knows.

Acknowledgements

Thank you to the following publications: *Butcher's Dog, Lighthouse, Eggbox, Durham Review of Books* and *The Great Northern Review*. Special thanks to Steve Mallon for his generous feedback and attention regarding early drafts of these poems. Credit to John Berryman's 'Olympus' which provided the inspiration for '15.' Thank you to my family, syndicated American television, British National Health Services, my cat Chappy, and the ghost orchid; an impetus for this cycle of poetic essays. Thank you to the following people, who helped more than they could possibly know: Arthur Allen, Aimee Elizabeth Skelton, Mark Flanagan, Jane McKie, Jen McConnell, Josh Mckee and Isabella Darcy Thomas-Kelly, and finally to Maria, who makes everything possible.

Haunt your unrest

Milton Keynes UK
Ingram Content Group UK Ltd.
UKHW042022040124
435397UK00003B/36